Soft Skills Sleuths

WORK ETHIC

Investigating Life Skills Success

Diane Lindsey Reeves with Connie Hansen
Illustrations by Ruth Bennett

CHERRY LAKE PRESS

Published in the United States of America by Cherry Lake Publishing Group
Ann Arbor, Michigan
www.cherrylakepublishing.com

Created and produced by Bright Futures Press
www.brightfuturespress.com

Reading Advisor: Marla Conn, MS, Ed., Literacy specialist, Read-Ability, Inc.
Illustrator: Ruth Bennett
Cover and Page Designer: Kathy Heming
Design Elements: © mijatmijatovic/Shutterstock.com; © GoodStudio/Shutterstock.com; © Denis Cristo/Shutterstock.com; © Lorelyn Medina/Shutterstock.com; © Yaroshenko Olena/Shutterstock.com; © rangsan paidaen/Shutterstock.com

Cherry Lake Press is an imprint of Cherry Lake Publishing Group.

Library of Congress Cataloging-in-Publication Data has been filed and is available at catalog.loc.gov

Cherry Lake Publishing Group would like to acknowledge the work of the Partnership for 21st Century Learning, a Network of Battelle for Kids. Please visit http://www.battelleforkids.org/networks/p21 for more information.

Printed in the United States of America
Corporate Graphics

TABLE OF CONTENTS

What Are Soft Skills and

Skills are needed to succeed at any job you can imagine. Different jobs require different skills. Professional baseball players need good batting and catching skills. Brain surgeons need steady hands and lots of practice with a scalpel. These are examples of **hard skills** necessary to do specific jobs.

Everyone needs "**soft skills**" to succeed in life. Soft skills get personal. They are about how you behave and treat people. Soft skills are the skills you need to be the very best *you* at home, work, and school.

"Sounds good," you say. "But I don't have a job. Why do I need to worry about soft skills?"

Ahh, but you do have a job. In fact, you have a very important job. You are a student, and your job is to learn as much as you can. Learning soft skills makes you a better student now. It also gets you ready to succeed in any career you choose later.

Work Ethic is about giving everything you do your best effort. It means coming through on tasks, chores, and assignments. Parents, teachers, and employers know they can count on someone with a strong work ethic to get things done and done well.

In this book, you get to be a soft skills **sleuth**. You will track down clues about what good (and not so good!) ethics skills look like. You will **investigate** four work ethic soft skills cases about what it is like to show:

- **Cooperation**
- **Respect**
- **Productivity**
- **Honesty**

Why Do I Need Them?

HOW TO USE THIS BOOK

Here's how you can be a soft skills sleuth. In each chapter:

- **Gather the facts.** Read the description about the soft skill.
- **Read the case file.** Check out a situation where soft skills are needed.
- **Investigate the case.** Look for clues showing soft skills *successes* and soft skills *mistakes*. Keep track of the clues on a blank sheet of paper.
- **Crack the case.** Did you spot all the clues?

SOFT SKILL #1

Rules, rules, rules! Families have them. Schools have them. Even games that are supposed to be fun have them. There is no escaping the fact that life is full of rules. **Cooperation** means that you follow rules wherever you are—at home, at school, and everywhere you go.

Cooperation is a choice. But it's also an attitude. It means you gladly work with others to accomplish a specific purpose. For instance, you obey traffic rules to keep roads safe. You clean up your room when your parents tell you to because it makes your home a nicer place to live. You cooperate without complaining, talking back, or showing a bad attitude.

Rules are meant to make things better, not harder. Can you imagine what your school would be like without rules? It wouldn't take long for the whole place to go crazy! Right? No one would learn anything, and school would be no fun.

Sure, it can be hard to obey rules sometimes. Try to remember that rules are usually a good thing. Cooperation is a big way to say thank you!

Ways to Cooperate at Home and School

- Obey rules that your parents, teachers, and other leaders set for you.
- Respect other people's space and belongings.
- Help out with chores and keep your space tidy.
- Figure out problems without arguing with other people.
- Keep your energy level calm and controlled.
- Show appreciation when others do nice things for you.

"I think life is a matter of choices, and that wherever we are, good or bad, is because of choices we make."
—Lou Holtz

COOPERATION

SOFT SKILLS CASE #1: COOPERATION

What's the first rule of the day for every student everywhere? Be on time! The day goes better when everyone shows up on time and ready to learn. It sets the tone for the whole day.

Ms. Poole likes it when her students follow this important rule. Will she find cooperative students in her classroom this morning? Turn the page and find out!

DO: Investigate cooperation successes and mistakes!

DO NOT: Write in this book!

School starts at 8:00 a.m. sharp! It's now 8:07 a.m. Is everyone ready to start the day? Which students are being cooperative? Which ones are not?

DID COOPERATION SHOW UP ON TIME?

COOPERATION

Is Ms. Poole's class off to a good start? How does breaking the rules make it harder for everyone?

Did you find all the successes and MISTAKES?

Start here!

Mistake.
Tardy! Everyone is waiting.

Success!
Hurray to two cooperative students in back.

Mistake.
Students sit in chairs, homework sits on desks.

Mistake.
Getting the morning off to a messy start.

CASE NOTES

How can you cooperate more at school and at home?

Mistake.
Bye-bye, cell phone.

Mistake.
Wake up, kid!

Did you find them all?

Success!
Sitting at desk. Homework ready. This student is ready to roll.

Mistake.
What's with the messy desk?

Mistake.
Starting homework now won't cut it.

SOFT SKILL #2

Speaking of rules, one of the most important rules in life is the Golden Rule. It goes like this: treat other people the way you want them to treat you. That is how you show **respect**. You treat people well and speak to them in nice ways.

Respect acts, sounds, and feels different than disrespect. Respectful behavior is kind and helpful. It sounds polite. When you treat someone with respect, you both feel good. The opposite is true for disrespect. It is selfish and even mean. It sounds sassy and full of bad attitude. A *disrespectful* person may not feel bad, but a *disrespected* person certainly does!

Respect works best when you share it with everyone you meet. It doesn't matter how important or popular a person is. It doesn't matter their age, race, or background. All people deserve to be treated with **dignity** and respect.

And that includes you! It is hard to respect others when you don't respect yourself. Be sure to turn the Golden Rule inside out: treat yourself the way you want others to treat you. Self-respect means that you like yourself. You treat yourself the same way you would treat your best friend.

Ten Ways to Show Respect

- Be a good listener.
- Be an encourager.
- Be kind.
- Be polite.
- Be thankful.
- Be helpful.
- Be responsible.
- Be fair.
- Be generous.
- Be trustworthy.

"Respect yourself, and others will respect you."
—Confucius

RESPECT

SOFT SKILLS CASE #2: RESPECT

It's lunchtime, and there are lots of hungry students in the cafeteria. Everyone knows the drill. Go through the lunch line, find a seat, and enjoy a good lunch. At least that's the way it's supposed to happen. It only works when everyone shows respect for each other, the staff, and themselves.

It's time for a respect reality check! Turn the page to find out who's using it and who isn't.

DO:
Investigate respect successes and mistakes!

DO NOT:
Write in this book!

Where is the Golden Rule when you need it most? How is—and isn't—it being used in this cafeteria scene?

IS RESPECT ON THE MENU?

RESPECT

Which students are showing respect in the cafeteria? Which ones need to mind their manners?

Did you find all the successes and MISTAKES?

Start here!

Mistake.
Giving the lunch lady a hard time.

Success!
Cleaning up after yourself shows respect.

Mistake.
Show some respect! If it's not yours, don't take it!

Success!
Smart food choices show self-respect.

Mistake.
Food fight. What a mess.

CASE NOTES

How do you show r-e-s-p-e-c-t?

Success!
Thanks for waiting your turn.

Mistake.
Junk food disses your body.

Did you find them all?

Success!
Saying please and thank you makes everyone feel good.

Success!
Helping a friend in need is good indeed.

Success!
Spill something? No problem when you clean it up.

SOFT SKILL #3

Sports coaches sometimes describe players as being "on top of their game." That means they are working hard, learning new things, and giving the game their very best efforts. In other words, they are being **productive**.

The most successful people in life are productive people. When you are productive, you get the job done. You don't wait for someone to make you do what you are supposed to do. You are a **self-starter**. You want to do the task, and you want to do it well. In other words, you are **driven**.

Productive people plan and set goals. When you have a task to do, you don't put it off. You get to it and do it! That way, problems turn into challenges that you can solve.

Focus is one way to stay productive. Focus keeps you from trying to do too much at once. It's when, for example, you are working on your math homework, your science fair project, and your book report at the same time. You need to focus on one thing at a time!

Productive students pay attention in class. They do their homework. They put in extra effort on special reports and projects. Productive students build habits that will always serve them well.

A Few Ways to Be Productive

- Tackle your hardest tasks first.
- Stay away from distractions like TV, cell phones, and loud noise.
- Break big jobs into small tasks.
- Finish what you start.
- Come up with good solutions to problems.

PRODUCTIVITY

SOFT SKILLS CASE #3: PRODUCTIVITY

It's time for the science fair. Students have been preparing for this day all semester. At least, that was what they were supposed to do. Some students have worked hard and given the projects lots of thought and effort. Some students look like they are throwing things together at the last minute.

Can you tell which students are "on top of their productivity game?"

DO:
Investigate productivity successes and mistakes!

DO NOT:
Write in this book!

WHO WINS THE PRIZE FOR PRODUCTIVITY?

The proof of productivity is in the results! Which science projects show signs of productive effort?
1st
HAMPSTER POWER
Flying Fish

PRODUCTIVITY

Everyone shared the same goal: create a good science project. Some students were productive. Others . . . not so much.

Did you find all the successes and MISTAKES?

Start here!

Mistake.
Last-minute excuses about "invisible" projects doesn't cut it.

Success!
Three cheers for the hamster project!

Success!
Someone's project is flying high.

Mistake.
Goofing around instead of getting the job done.

CASE NOTES

Mistake.
"Forgetting" your project at home.

Mistake.
Missing the deadline.

How can you be more productive at home and school?

Did you find them all?

Success!
Working together makes big tasks more fun.

Mistake.
Following directions prevents disasters.

Mistake.
Waiting until the last minute to set up.

SOFT SKILL #4

Honesty shows up in two ways. It shows up in what you say and in what you do. Honest people tell the truth. Dishonest people tell lies. Being an honest person means that you admit when you make a mistake or get into trouble. You do this even when it would be easier to lie your way out of it.

Cheating and stealing are examples of dishonest actions. Cheating means acting unfairly to gain an advantage. Copying someone else's work on a test is one way that some people cheat. Stealing is taking something that doesn't belong to you.

When people lie, cheat, or steal, they hurt others as well as themselves. They rob themselves of a good **reputation** or image. They become known by their dishonest words and actions. Other people think twice before trusting them with anything important.

When others know they can count on you to be honest, it builds trust. People like honest people better. Honest people like themselves better too!

Honesty Means That You...

- Own up to your mistakes.
- Don't make promises you cannot keep.
- Make sure your actions match your words.
- Think before you speak.
- Catch yourself when telling **white lies**, and stop.
- Do your own work.
- Can be who you really are without having to fake it.

"Success doesn't count unless you earn it fair and square."
—Michelle Obama

HONESTY

SOFT SKILLS CASE #4: HONESTY

Honesty gets put to the test every day in so many ways. It may look like just another day in art class for the students shown on the following pages. But the truth is that these students have to make lots of choices about speaking and acting honestly.

Take a look at the art class scene on the next page. Can you tell who is proving that honesty is the best policy?

DO:
Investigate honesty successes and mistakes!

DO NOT:
Write in this book!

CAN YOU SPOT THE DIFFERENCES?

These young artists are letting their creative talents loose. Some are creating masterpieces. Others are making a mess of their reputations by stealing, cheating, or not telling the truth.

THE ART OF HONESTY

HONESTY

Some students are working in honest ways. Some are not. Which students are showing honesty? Which ones are not?

Did you find all the successes and MISTAKES?

Start here!

Mistake.
Hey! Those art supplies don't belong to you.

Success!
Pitching in to help clean up.

Mistake.
Saying "it's not my fault" when it actually is.

CASE NOTES

How can you be true to yourself?

Mistake.
Put your name on your own painting, kid!

Success!
Taking responsibility for your own mistakes.

Did you find them all?

Mistake.
Speak truth or don't speak at all.

Success!
Honest feedback is best served with kindness.

Success!
Taking pride in a job well done.

WHAT HAVE YOU Learned?

WORK ETHIC QUIZ

Question 1:

People with a strong ________ ________ get their work done and done well.

Question 2:

Cooperation means following the ________________.

Question 3:

The ____________ ____________ says "treat others the way you'd like them to treat you."

Question 4:

It is important to treat ________________ with respect.

Question 5:

Successful people are ____________ people.

Question 6:

One way to be productive is to ____________ on one task at a time.

Question 7:

Honesty means to tell the ____________.

Question 8:

Lying, ____________, and ____________ are all ways to be dishonest.

ANSWERS

1. *work ethic*
2. *rules*
3. *Golden Rule*
4. *all people or everyone*
5. *productive*
6. *focus*
7. *truth*
8. *cheating, stealing*

Work ethic soft skills start here!

GLOSSARY

cooperation (koh-ah-pur-AY-shuhn) the action of being helpful by doing what is wanted or asked for; following the rules

dignity (DIG-nih-tee) the quality that makes a person worthy of honor or respect

driven (DRIV-in) hardworking and ambitious

ethics (ETH-iks) the moral code that guides a person's choices about right and wrong

hard skills (HAHRD SKILZ) specific skills needed to do a specific job

honesty (AH-nis-tee) truthfulness and sincerity no matter what

hydrated (HYE-dray-tid) having consumed enough water or other liquid

investigate (in-VES-tih-gate) to gather information or clues about something

productive (pruh-DUHK-tiv) accomplishing a lot work

reputation (rep-yuh-TAY-shuhn) how other people regard someone or something

respect (rih-SPEKT) high regard shown for someone or something

responsible (rih-SPAHN-suh-buhl) accepting the duty to take care of someone or something

self-starter (SELF STAHR-tur) someone who is able to work on their own

sleuth (SLOOTH) a detective, or person who is good at finding facts and clues

soft skills (SAWFT SKILZ) behaviors and personality traits people use every day to succeed in life

stress (STRES) the feeling of being worried or overwhelmed

white lies (WITE LYEZ) false comments about a little or unimportant matter

INDEX

ABOUT THE AUTHORS

Diane Lindsey Reeves likes to write books that help students figure out what they want to be when they grow up. She mostly lives in Washington, D.C., but spends as much time as she can in North Carolina and South Carolina with her grandkids.

Connie Hansen spent 25 years teaching college students about successful life skills. She lives in Lynchburg, Virginia where her favorite thing to do is play with her grandchildren. Her happy place is the beach!

ABOUT THE ILLUSTRATOR

Ruth Bennett lives in a small country village in the heart of Norfolk, England, with her two cats, Queen Elizabeth and Queen Victoria. She loves petting dogs, watching movies, and drawing, of course!